The Memo
You Got This!!!
-Life

Morgan,
I'm so proud of you
Go Forth & Change
the WORLD!!!
We Need You!

~ Ms. Sampson
A.K.A
Sonia B.

The Memo
You Got This!!!
-Life

Amethyst Paradox Publishing

Amethyst Paradox Publishing
PO Box 10476
Rochester, New York 14610

The Memo

Copyright © 2019 by Sonia Begonia. All rights reserved.

Cover Design By S-SQUARED DESIGNS

This book or parts thereof may not be reproduced in any form, stored in a retrieval system, or transmitted in any form or by any means - electronic, mechanical, photocopy, recording, or otherwise - without the prior written permission of the author, Sonia Begonia; cover designer, S-Squared Designs; or the publisher, Amethyst Paradox Publishing, except as provided by United States of America copyright law. For permission requests, write to the publisher, at "Attention: Permissions Coordinator", at the address above or email at:
legal@amethystparadoxbooks.com

For information about special discounts for bulk purchase, email:
bulk.orders@amethystparadoxbooks.com

First Printing: 2018

ISBN - 13: 978-1-7325186-0-5 (paperback)
ISBN - 13: 978-1-7325186-1-2 (eBook)

Library of Congress Control Number: 2018952767 (print & eBook)

10 9 8 7 6 5 4 3 2 1

First Edition Printed in the United States of America

This is for all of my students:
past, present, and future

The Memo

You Got This!!!
-Life

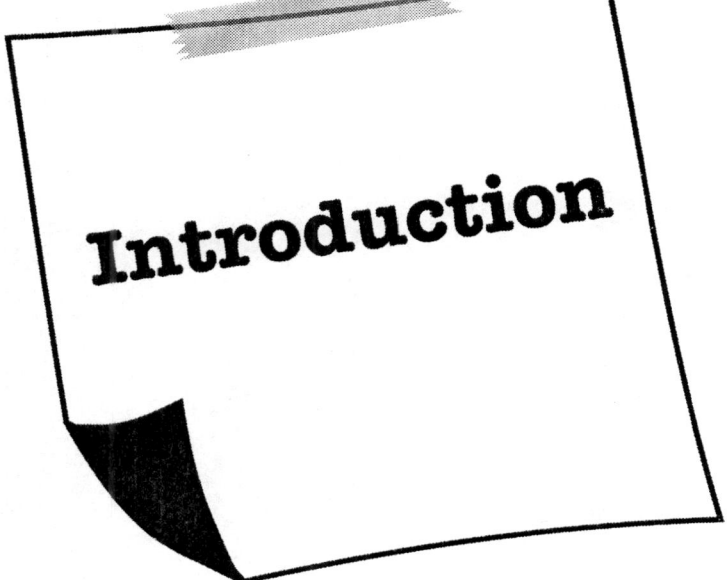

Adulting
a·dul·ting
/uh-duhl-tiŋ/

Verb

1 : of or relating to being an adult

2 : of or relating to activities typically designated for persons over the age of 18

3 : showing a level of responsibility, ingenuity, and self-determination to accomplish goals and responsibilities related to being an adult

Congratulations!!! You are an adult now! (What? Whaaat!!! #ImGrownNow #GrownAF) Like a full-fledged, no-holds-barred, Adult. You now have all of the rights, privileges, benefits, but most importantly, the responsibilities of being an adult. You are now responsible for every facet of your life. You no longer have mommy, daddy, auntie, uncle, grandma, grandpa, or whatever adult(s) you have in your life taking responsibility for you and your well-being. You are NOW the newest fish in the adult ocean. You can either swim riding the current or you can get swept away and go belly up.

Luckily, you don't have to go at it blindly. You have a life preserver of sorts...well, more like a lighthouse. I will help you navigate through these rough few years so you don't hit the rocks that I did. Now if you want to be hardheaded and not follow my advice, that is on you. Screw your life up...I really don't care (unless it interferes with my life - then I got to cut 'cha!). But enough of the craziness. Find a good spot to sit down so you can fully engross yourself in this book. You're an adult now...and you can't afford to mess up!!!

From time to time, I may use a little profanity. There is a responsibility one must have when using profanity. RULE #1: NEVER USE PROFANITY IN VAIN! Don't use F-bombs just because you can, use them because they give emphasis and clarity to what you are saying. The use of profanity is a privilege. If you don't do it right, I will take that privilege from you!

At the same time, I will not use profanity in vain. If I have it in there, trust and believe there is a purpose for it. I have a plethora of vocabulary words that I could use but sometimes, just sometimes, the use of profanity has a purpose!

And that right there is my profanity disclaimer!

Shall we continue?!? Ok...Good!!!

There aren't instructions with color coded pictures handcrafted by the universe carefully articulating adultness to help you "build" your adult life. There isn't a Supplies List telling you what you will need. There isn't an 800 number that you can call that will tell you what to do when you get stuck. Luckily, you (or someone close to you) got this here book to help you out. To give you a little guidance so life won't be so "new". This book will help prepare you to grab life by the horns and kick its whole ass to success!

This book is broken down into 7 memos:
1. Adulting Basics
2. Who Are You?
3. End Game Mentality
4. Preparedness
5. #SquadGoals
6. Advocacy
7. Be You, ALWAYS

MAKE SURE YOU READ ALL SEVEN MEMOS! I know they say reading is fundamental but you don't know how many times people win or lose because of their willingness or unwillingness to read. This includes employee handbooks, a syllabus in class, those pesky instructions to assemble that new piece of furniture, and the list goes on.

So read up, enjoy, and be great!

When you need that 30-second crash course because you have so much going on and you just want/need a checklist of the things you need to do and/or accomplish, that's this section. Check out the **RESOURCES SECTION** for more information and to begin your search/research. Make sure you do your research to find the best option for you. I hope you didn't think I was just going to spoon-feed you all of the answers...that's no fun. And as a teacher, if that is what I was going to do, I wouldn't be doing my job in preparing you for Adulthood.

Here's your quick checklist of things that need to be taken care of within the next 6 months:

1. Purchase a small safe (this will be crucial in keeping your valuables and documents secure)
    Requirements:
    - Waterproof (minimum of 72 hours)
    - Fireproof (up to 1550°F for 30 minutes, minimum)
    - Drop-proof (at least 2 stories)
2. Purchase a POWER suit (charcoal grey, grey, and/or navy)
3. Register to vote
4. Updated Resume

SAFE
As you begin your journey into adulthood these items will help you secure yourself. The safe will keep the necessary documents you are going to get (see the DOCUMENTS section on page 13) safe and secure from theft as well as fire. The right safe will also make it impossible for someone to drop your safe from specific heights (say 2 or 3 stories) in order to bust the safe open. INVEST the money in having peace of mind.

SUIT
When purchasing a power suit, purchase a classic/timeless suit (don't trend out your power suit). Most importantly, purchase a suit that is perfect for your body type. GET THE SUIT TAILORED!!! Having an ill-fitting suit speaks volumes to potential employers about you that you didn't even consider. Find an amazing tailor that will have you looking and feeling like the billionaire you want to become.

VOTING
Sometimes I wonder if I really need to explain to you why you need to register to vote, but I am going to anyway. Time and time again we are reminded of the power of the ballot (whether we choose to exercise that right or not). I am not going to tell you which (if any) party to be affiliated. That is a decision you need to come to ON YOUR OWN based on your core principles and the research you have done. But I will say this, your local elected officials will do more for you (good or bad) than the president... make sure you research them, their policies, their belief systems, and if they have held an office before, their record. Don't vote just to say you voted, and don't vote for particular candidates because they are in the party you have aligned with. Vote for the candidate you feel best aligns with your core principles and can do the best job in that office.

RESUME

For the love of GAWD...please update your resume every 6 months. There are new skills that you learn on the job, at school, in life, etc. Let the record reflect your awesomeness!!! And if you need someone to look over your resume, hit me up. I'll look it over and make you look like the kick ass rock star employee that employers want to employ!!!

Documents

- State identification and/or drivers' license
- Copy of your birth certificate
- Social security card
- Passport
- AARP membership
- AAA membership

This is gonna be brief since I got extra longwinded already...just get these documents. They are important and necessary for YOU (not ya mama, or ya daddy, or grandma, or ya auntie) to have in your possession. AND FOR THE LOVE OF ALL THINGS HOLY... PUT THEM IN THE SAFE THAT YOU PURCHASED EARLIER!!! Don't say I have never done anything for you!

Don't judge me with the AARP membership. I am under 40 and I have had one since I was in my 20s. It's the best decision I've made. It is cheaper than AAA membership and has amazing discounts from hotels and car rentals to restaurants and glasses. Don't get it twisted though, AAA has great member benefits as well so get that too.

Insurance
- Medical
- Health Insurance
- Supplemental Insurance (think: Aflac)
- Car
- Renters (this is a MUST if you are renting)
- Life Insurance (think about beneficiaries)

MEDICAL
Please do the research on these insurance companies. Many medical insurance companies have websites and apps you can use to check to see which doctors accept which insurances. If you think you are going out of town or even out of state for school, call your insurance company to see if your insurance works in that new location. If not, work with the adults in your life to get the insurance that works in that area. There's nothing worse than getting the school designated insurance. So you have two scenarios, you either pay for two insurances so you can be insured in your new location OR you can use your insurance that is considered OUT OF NETWORK and pay helluva lot more for standard services. OR you can do like I said and get insurance that works in multiple locations.

AUTO
When you are looking for car insurance make sure that at the very least you are getting your state minimum requirements for insurance. However, I'd recommend that you get the most you can afford. The last thing you need to happen is having to come out of pocket for an accident. Not all insurance companies are created equal, but it isn't too hard to find the best bang for your buck. The internet makes it much easier to do side-by-side comparisons but always, ALWAYS, ALWAYS give them a call. There are things that a live person can finagle that you won't be able to get from the internet.

So...CALL 'EM UP AND TELL EM WHAT YOU WANT!!!

Word of Advice: DO AUTOPAY!!! I made the mistake of not doing that and unbeknownst to me, my policy was cancelled because I paid it, but it never went through. Policy got cancelled and car registration was suspended.

RENTERS

If you are renting, GET RENTERS INSURANCE!!! There's nothing worse than "the worst things" happening. Without it you can lose everything with no recourse to get anything back. Please make sure you take pictures of your belongings for insurance purposes. Write a list of all the books, music, movies, and other REPLACEABLE items that you have. Put them in that safe you purchased earlier. Also, writing down all of your technology's model and serial numbers is a must. This ensures that if anything is lost or stolen, you can give this information to the police and your insurance company.

Medical
- Apply for insurance or get your own copy of your insurance card
- Pick your own medical personnel
  - Internist (I prefer an internist over a general practioner)
  - OB/GYN
  - Dentist
  - Chiropractor
  - Massage therapist
  - Mental health professional
  - Endocrinologist (if needed)
  - Allergist (if needed)
  - ENT [Ear, Nose, Throat] (if needed)
  - Urologist (if needed)
  - Pulmonologist (if needed)
  - Cardiologist (if needed)

It is VERY IMPORTANT that you have a copy of your insurance card. This is your "passport" to a better and healthier you. Give them a call and get a thorough understanding of your plans benefits and limitations. Ask questions until you are tired of asking questions, then call back and ask more.

You need to know what services you can and cannot receive, where you can go to receive those services, and who can provide them. ALWAYS, ALWAYS, ALWAYS choose in-network doctors or you will find yourself with a hefty medical bill you may not be able to pay off!

Most importantly, don't let these doctors punk you. You own that doctor, advocate for yourself. Be the champion for you. Stick around and I'll show you how to OWN those doctors' appointments and get the proper medical care FOR YOU!

FYI: PLEASE, PLEASE, PLEASE...do not take an ambulance if you do not have to. Who has $500 to pay for an ambulance? Yup that's right...$500 for a ride to the hospital!!!

Financial
- Get a financial planner
- Credit Score/Reports
- Bank Accounts (checking, savings, CDs, MMA, online savings, etc.)
- Create a monthly budget

So this is the part where I indulge and actually give you some information. Finances require a little bit more attention. I am going to only give you a small taste because, best believe I will be coming out with an ENTIRE book about finances. LAWD knows I messed up enough with my finances to give you the warnings of what NOT to do.

FINACIAL PLANNER
When I say get a financial planner...GET THE BLOODY FINANCIAL PLANNER. This is NOT a suggestion, this is NOT a request, IT'S A MANDATE!!! You will thank me later. HOWEVER, I will advise you to do your research and make sure you are getting a financial planner that knows what they are doing. One who has taken the time to be knowledgeable and stays abreast with all of the new nuances of credit scores and reporting, financial markets, credit markets, etc.

CREDIT REPORTS/SCORES
Credit reports and scores are so important. They track your financial habits and help institutions predict whether or not you will be able to borrow money from them and pay them back (think: loans, mortgage, etc.). It not only affects whether entities will lend to you, but also how much they will lend and what is the interest rate on the loan, and even your rates for car insurance.

BANK ACCOUNT
Get a bank account. Find one that is FDIC (or NCUA if it is a credit union) insured. Find one that is convenient for you in all the places you frequent. If you are like me and travel to different cities and states (and even different countries) make sure your bank is accessible to you in those various places. In addition make sure they have the customer service you deserve and expect.

There are various accounts that you can get from a bank and/or credit union. I would recommend doing both. There are benefits for having your money at a bank and at a credit union. Don't forget about online banking. There are entities that provide online savings accounts and other accounts that are geared towards you managing your money as well as saving money.

MONTHLY BUDGET
Now is the time to secure your financial outlook by making sound financial decisions before it's too late. So create that budget. Figure out how much you need to live per month (expenses: food, car note, gas, loans, credit cards, entertainment, etc.) plus a savings plan. This will help you in securing your financial future.

Don't forget to check out the **RESOURCES** section. I believe it will help you in your adulting endeavor. I'm sure you are wondering why some of these items are there; that will be addressed in later sections of this book.

So we finally have the basics out of the way, time to get down and dirty and get our adulting on!

Today is my prep day...In the words of Leonidas, "Today we eat, for tomorrow we fight".

Resources:

Recommended Books:
The 7 Habits of Highly Effective People by Stephen R. Covey
The Alchemist by Paulo Coelho
The Dip by Seth Godin
The Fifth Agreement by Don Miguel Ruiz
The Four Agreements by Don Miguel Ruiz
The Turning Point by Malcolm Gladwell
The University of Hard Knocks by Ralph Parlette
Year of Yes by Shonda Rhimes

Links & Apps:
AAA: www.aaa.com
AARP: www.aarp.org
Birth Certificate: Your State's Department of Health
Credit Karma: www.creditkarma.com
Credit Reports & Scores: www.usa.gov/credit-reports
Credit Sesame: creditsesame.com
Equifax: www.equifax.com
Experian: www.experian.com
Free Credit Report: www.annualcreditreport.com
Hello Wallet: www.hellowallet.com
ID/Drivers License: Your State's DMV
Nerd Wallet: www.nerwallet.com
Passport: travel.state.gov/content/passports/en/passports.html
Social Security Card: www.ssa.gov/ssnumber
Transunion: www.transunion.com
Voting: www.usa.gov/register-to-vote or www.vote.gov

Originally, I was going to write this towards the end of the book. Then I thought about writing this at the beginning of the book. Only to conclude this needed to be in both the beginning and the end of the book. You are the Alpha and the Omega...the beginning and the end of your life story. I know there are some religious people side-eyeing me right now, but that's ok. I love ya anyhow!

I really need you to grasp the concept that this here thing is YOUR LIFE!!! Not your parents', not your friends', not your teachers', not even your past mistakes!!!

Say it with me: THIS IS MY LIFE!!! THIS IS MY LIFE!!!

THIS
IS
MY
LIFE!!!

So what does that even mean? What is YOUR LIFE?!?! Your life is what you make it, HOWEVER... let me repeat HOOOOW-EEEEVVVVEEEERRRR!!!!! You must have a purpose, vision, and/or mission for your life. So this memo of WHO ARE YOU? will be about you stating your purpose, your passion, your core principles, your self-mission, and your personal vision.

So, let's get down to business!

As you get older decisions have to be made. Some decisions are easy and some...not so much. Your moral compass is your decision maker when you can't make a decision. When you can't decide whether to go left or right, stay or leave, quit or press forward... your moral compass will help guide you through!

The process to developing one's moral compass is ongoing and it looks different for everyone, but it is a necessary process to begin and refine as you go through life. Now let me clarify, when I say refine I mean tweak and/or fine tune. Your moral compass shouldn't change based on life events. However, life events can help you understand why you have the moral compass you do and what you need to do to fortify your resolve to have the moral compass that you have.

Your moral compass is all inclusive. It is unwavering - translatable across life. No matter the situation it will guide you through, and to your best self. Your moral compass will help ease your mind and help you live your life without regrets. Your moral compass will not exempt you from thinking about the shouldas, wouldas, couldas in life but it will help you feel comfortable with your decision...knowing you not only did what was best for you but also you did so by aligning your decision with who you are at your core.

Your moral compass can incorporate religious beliefs, but it is not necessary to have religious beliefs in order to develop a moral compass. The components that make up your moral compass must be things you truly believe and can live out on a daily basis. Both when people are watching and when they are not!

Now this is our first memo so let me put you on to what happens next. After the gems and jewels have been dropped you have a **GET IT RIGHT, GET IT TIGHT** assignment. These assignments are what we, in the industry (educational industry that is), call low-stakes. That means that if you screw it up it won't be that big of a deal, there are no real stakes here (your life, lifestyle, livelihood, etc. are not on the line). So I introduce to you, your FIRST assignment:

GET IT RIGHT, GET IT TIGHT:

Your moral compass is <u>YOUR TRUTH</u>!!! Do not allow others to sway you from it! It is not your job or responsibility to convince anyone or explain to them your moral compass. It is your doctrine, it is your law. It is as flexible and/or as rigid as you want it to be. Don't bend or break it for anyone. Not your parents, your elders, your friends, significant (or insignificant) other, children, etc. Now understand that there may be consequences for the actions you take. Take those consequences with your head held high, confidence in your heart, and with peace of mind knowing you followed your moral compass even in the toughest situations.

So how do we create this magical doctrine that can and will help guide you through the perils of life? It's the most simplistically difficult thing you will ever have to do!!!

Your first step is trying to figure out the type of person you wish to be. This task will require the use of a dictionary. You are to pick 3 words that can be used to describe you based on the person you want to be (or even the person you are now).

I grew up in a Baptist (Christian) church. I was raised on the principles of Jesus. There were many things that I took away from those teachings. The main ones include being a disciple (student) - always learning, always wanting to grow - do better and be better; and being a genuinely good person - if I have, WE have. I will always look out for those around me, help those in need, be good to others, and show love; and bring light to wherever I go.

Unlike Judas, loyalty is everything. No exceptions. Money doesn't buy loyalty. Power desn't change loyalty. Even if I'm no longer with the person, friends with the person or speaking to the person - I still remain loyal. What does that mean? What was said to me in confidence remains in confidence. Just because they did me wrong doesn't mean I repay them in kind. I can't build up my character by destroying theirs!

Although these characteristics make up who I am, I chose the following words as the foundation of my moral compass: charity, love, strength, discernment, elegance, grace, and trust. These seven words help to point me in the direction that I am meant to go in. Here are three of the seven words in details I used to describe myself are:

1. <u>Elegance:</u> to exhibit good taste, amiability, equilibrium, and harmony in all my dealings, relationships, decisions, choices, goals, and lifestyle

2. <u>Grace:</u> To move and act with controlled, polite, and pleasant mannerisms,
To be smooth and attractive in actions, speech, and presentation

3. <u>Trust:</u> To be reliable, good, honest, and effective to myself and others

These help to make me (and keep me) as the "good" person that I am today. Let's not all act like mistakes and missteps don't happen. This takes time to work on, solidify, and continuously honing in on to develop into the person you wish to be.

MINI GET IT RIGHT, GET IT TIGHT:

Now it's your turn, what are your three words (don't forget definitions):

1. _____
_____
_____
_____
_____
_____
_____

2. _____
_____
_____
_____
_____
_____
_____

3. _____
_____
_____
_____
_____
_____
_____

Now think, what is your reasoning for choosing those words? Will people get it? Are your actions aligned to these characteristics and/or can you do the actions that will align to them? Can those three adjectives be used to create a personal manifesto?

Before you can move forward to write your Personal Manifesto, you need to understand exactly what it is. A manifesto (in the generalest of senses) is a public declaration of your principle of action and the direction (you know that moral compass thing is going to keep popping up) in which you hope to go.

So, let's look over those three words again.

1._____
_____
_____
_____

2._____
_____
_____
_____

3._____
_____
_____
_____

Are those three words strong enough for you to configure a manifesto? If yes, skip down to page 34. If no, let's keep working at it.

IF NO, START HERE:

One of the most difficult tasks is to self-reflect and determine who you are and/or who you want to be. What is even harder than that is to be more concise about those descriptors. The best way to think about the top three words to characterize your character is to think about the worst possible situation you could be in: going to prison, death of a loved one, dying from an incurable disease, or even your own death. It is during these moments (not the good times), that one's true character comes out. What do you want people to see in you? But most importantly, what do you want to see in yourself?

How do you want YOU to come out of all of these situations? Do you want your strength to come through, your compassion, your adaptability? Who ARE you? What are your redeeming qualities? What is the "thing" that will help you make the tough decisions for, let's say, pulling or not pulling the plug on a loved one? Whether or not you speak up or lay low? And not just what decisions you will make but also how you will deal with the consequences of those decisions later on. No one can sleep/live with the choices you make, only you can do that. So what words would you put to describe that decision-making process.

MINI GET IT RIGHT, GET IT TIGHT:

Let's look into the three most commonly used words that people like to describe their ideal self:
>Compassionate
>Caring
>Open-minded

I want you to break down these three words. Do a little etymology research...rediscover these words. See how these words aren't really COMPLETE. Now dig deeper, look ha'duh (in my Rafiki voice) and find words that describe your integrity. And with each word...ask yourself why you choose that word. Write out your thought process. Once you have completed that, go on to the next page and continue the process of writing your Personal Manifesto.

1._____

_____

_____

_____

2._____

_____

_____

_____

3._____

_____

_____

_____

IF YES, START HERE:

Now that we have figured out the descriptors that can help inform your Personal Manifesto let's work towards turning those words into statements and those statements into a manifesto. So, let us now focus on creating a written version of your character and contributions & achievements. This is my personal manifesto. I know I'll tweak it again soon.

My Manifesto of Greatness

My character is based on my integrity.
My integrity, my state of being - whole and undivided
is based on my core principles
These principles are: Elegance, Grace, Trust, Charity, Love, Strength, and Discernment.
These principles will guide my goals, values, and actions
These principles will help me to manage my time and my life.
They will inform me on how to prioritize and organize.
My principles will guide me into fulfilling my destiny and contributing positively to my life
and the lives of others.
My principles will be the driving force
to living the life of unapologetic happiness!

This is a principle-based manifesto. You don't have to write yours this way. You can write your manifesto in the affirmative (it is a fact and/or true). Affirmative statements can be I AM, I WILL, I MUST, etc. They are commands that you hold to be true and self-evident. They are commands that you internalize and then project to the world about who you are and your contributions to this world.

GET IT RIGHT, GET IT TIGHT:

You are going to write your manifesto. A manifesto is your statement to the world of who you are, what are your aims. How do you want people to see you?
So let us know who you are...and GO!!!

End-Game Mentality

I LOVE SCANDAL!!! I am the biggest OPA (Olivia Pope & Associates) fan, EVER! The show was created based on Judith Smith, a real life "fixer". Any good fixer works toward not just "squashing" bad situations but finding the best possible outcome for her client. One of the many things that I love about the Olivia Pope character is her methodology in helping her clients. Her method of gleaning from her clients what it is they wish to realize, gain, achieve, eliminate, etc. from their situation and/or opportunity. Before she 'makes it do what it do', she asks her clients two simple questions:

>What do you want?
>What is your end game?

So now you must become your own fixer and figure out the "silver lining" in any situation.

Typically, when people ask us "what do you want?" We can answer more in the negative (I don't want this, I don't want that) than in the positive (I want this, I want that). But in order to get what we want, because as humans that's the goal...to get what YOU WANT! you need to know what you want. When you were a baby to get what you wanted you screamed, cried and hollered. As a toddler you threw temper tantrums to get what you wanted. As an adult, those tactics do not work. You have to learn to articulate your wants and needs in terms that you know what is what and in terms OTHERS can understand.

Knowing what you want, knowing how the "story" ends will help you figure out the solution to the problems that you will face in life. Knowing your destination makes creating the roadmap easier. It also helps you to overcome any roadblocks and/or detours that you WILL come up against in reaching your destination. Knowing what you want (or where you are going) can help you determine whether the course of action you are taking makes sense. It empowers you to make decisions to stop and reroute (some people will call it quitting, I call it rerouting) yourself without feeling guilty for that decision.

Truth be told, that is how I was able to write this book. I asked myself, what did I want people to get from reading this book. I also thought about the different things that I wish someone would have sat down with me and discussed. Life isn't ever going to "be easy" but knowing what you want and having a plan to get there makes life a little bit easier. But I digress.

Now figuring out your destination takes some introspection. In any situation you have to think about your end game and act accordingly. Here are the three simple rules to the end-game mentality:
>   RULE #1: DO NOT LIE!
>   RULE #2: SET GOALS
>   RULE #3: RE-EVALUATE

Rule #1: DO NOT LIE!

When trying to figure out what you want, don't lie to others and most definitely don't lie to yourself. That does not help you accomplish your goals. Be true to yourself. Never do anything for others - in the sense of allowing people to live vicariously through you versus doing things for the upliftment and edification of the human race - the latter is always worth doing - always do them for you.

Rule #2: SET GOALS!
When setting goals you have to think of the other two questions that OPA asks their clients:

What do you want that you can ACTUALLY have?

What do you want that's POSSIBLE?

Many people will tell you to create **S.M.A.R.T.** Goals. **S.M.A.R.T.** Goals was first referenced in 1981 by George T. Doran and typically associated with Peter Drucker. **S.M.A.R.T.** is an acronym for Specific, Measurable, Attainable, Realistic, and Time-bound. It is a great tool to use when creating accomplishable goals. Since this book is about adulting, we are going to create **A.D.U.L.T.** Goals. I am going to give you this information now, but it will all make sense for application when you read the memo: ADVOCACY

A.D.U.L.T. Goals

A: stands for applicable (does it apply to your life)

D: stands for definable (specific and measurable)

U: stands for useful (beneficial)

L: stands for likely to happen (is this attainable)

T: stands for timetable (deadlines)

When creating goals the goals you create must be applicable to you and your situation/life. Don't go around just creating goals for yourself because you say so-and-so on somebody's social media page do it and they were successful at it. If it doesn't apply to you and what you want to do long-term. If it doesn't help you showcase your personal mission, if it is not helping you exhibit your core beliefs...it is NOT, I repeat, IT IS NOT APPLICABLE TO YOU! That means, simply put, don't waste your time!

Once it has been determined that this goal/objective is applicable to you, it's now time to define the goal. Can you articulate with specificity and measurability the goal you want to accomplish? Time to get your pen and paper out to write out the goal, break down its different components, determine how success is going to be measured, and the various forms of accountability you are going to give yourself to accomplish said goal.

After that is done, you need to look over the goal and ask yourself is this goal USEFUL? What will come of me accomplishing this goal? If this can't be answered, it is time to start all over, go back to the drawing board and figure the usefulness factor out. Otherwise, it will be just another thing wasting your time. And unlike money, time is a commodity you can't get back.

So your goal has proven to be applicable, definable, and useful. Now it has to be determined if it is likely to happen. Think about the definition of your goal, your measurement of success, your forms of accountability as well as your timetable. Do you need to adjust anything to make this goal happen?

Last but not least, your goal has to have a timetable. The difference between a dream and a goal is a deadline. I've dreamed of becoming a published author, however, it wasn't until I gave myself a deadline that I actually succeeded in becoming a published author.

WARNING: Just because you followed the steps, doesn't mean it will be a clear path to success. Shit happens and deadlines come and go and the goal hasn't even been started yet (I've had SEVERAL deadlines for this book that came and left). It's OKAY!!! Just keep pushing, assess why deadlines were missed, identify where you can use assistance, and GET THAT HELP!!!

Rule #3: RE-EVALUATE

One of the major steps people forget to do as they are goal slaying is re-evaluating. As life goes on, we need to look at the goals we set, the steps we are taking to accomplish them and re-evaluate what and how we are doing this. We need to look at the new knowledge that we acquired and notice the different options that become available. We must determine whether or not these options are worthy of consideration when it comes to goal accomplishment. Re-evaluation is the key to effective and efficient goal completion but most importantly, it is the key to determining if the goals we set are aligned with who we are and how we present that to the world.

Now understand this, although I am writing this book, please believe I didn't always have all the answers - and let's be honest, I still don't. I messed up, royally, many times throughout my life. It's not the fuck ups that matter, it's what you do afterwards that counts. I really hate the phrase: If I could do it all over again I would change this, that, and the third. Well guess what, you can't, so get over it and move on! So here is my shining example of a story of how I didn't have the end in mind, what I lost out on, and how I learned to be more strategic in my dealings.

Let's take a trip back in time. I'm in my early twenties and ready to graduate. I had just come back to school from my winter break and I was on a mission to smash the semester. I had a class that was supposed to meet up once a week. I'm waiting to get updated information from the professor about the class, 3 weeks go by and NOTHING!!!! I have gone to the instructor's office, left notes and nothing. I finally email the instructor at the end of January (after the first three weeks of not hearing anything from the instructor). You know when I got a response? MARCH...yup that's right, in March almost 2 months later. Now my instructor wants me to come to the office like I am NOT on Spring Break...across the country!!!

By the time I came back from vacation, needless to say my pissedofftivity (yes that is a word...it's printed isn't it!) levels were on an all time high. I get to the office and the instructor basically changed the curriculum of the course and has the students working on the instructor's research. >Now this is when things start to go left< I was not having any parts of the instructor's research. I had worked on a different research topic (which is bomb.com) and I wasn't going to waste all of my hard work on this instructor's research.

Because I am about that life, I jumped out guns blazing not even considering what it is that I was really upset about and what I ultimately wanted. Without the use of profanity (because this was my instructor) I wrote a very scathing email. I called my instructor incompetent and everything else academically degrading and who cared my instructor has a doctorate degree. I was about that gully life. My instructor wanted to see if I was gonna jump and didn't know how high I would go with this. I was so upset I even ranted to one of my other instructors. I think I went to that class once the entire semester.

Later in the semester I go to the dean's office for something unrelated to the issue and the dean brings up the issue about my instructor. You know I'm like wow, I didn't even think the problem was as big as it was, thankfully my other instructor understood the magnitude of what was going on and told the dean what happened. The dean and I discussed it and I received an incomplete for the semester.

My friends thought I was nuts for going off on the instructor like that. I, on the other hand, understood the power I had as a student. I knew what could and couldn't happen to me and I played my hand pretty well (at least I thought I did). The instructor (who I forgot to mention was the chair of the undergraduate department – yeah coming for the person at the top like this is Game of Thrones) ended up being relieved of all undergraduate department chair responsibilities. You know I was smelling myself, can't you tell?!?

I was all little munchkins singing DING DONG THE WITCH IS DEAD about the situation until I STILL had to write the stupid research topic that the instructor gave. Although I "won" I also became a major loser in this situation. Had I thought about what I wanted in this situation, I could have gotten what I wanted.

End-game strategy was the lesson learned from this situation. Not only that, but you have more allies than you think. I never once considered tapping into that allyship to achieve my goals. I never gave the dean the benefit of the doubt in being able to assist me in accomplishing my goals. I fought that battle ALONE and I ALONE suffered the academic consequences of my actions. I knew my instructor couldn't fail me, but I knew I wouldn't have gotten a good grade on the assignment.

This was a lesson in knowing your end game in order to make CALCULATED steps to achieve your goal. Had a sat down and done my **A.D.U.L.T.** Goal for this situation, not only could I have gotten what I wanted, but I would have been prepared to complete what I wanted, how I wanted in a timeframe that was mutually agreed upon. In addition, this was also a lesson in advocacy, I advocated for myself (definitely not in the best possible way) without hesitation. We will discuss advocacy in a later portion of this book but NEVER be afraid to stand in your own truth and OWN it!

Ok, memo is done. I hope you took some great notes (I was definitely a gem dropper with this one)!!! I am sure you are ready to get this show on the road so here is your **GET IT RIGHT, GET IT TIGHT**.

GET IT RIGHT, GET IT TIGHT:

Situation: You have goal of _____
_____ (fill in the blank). What are the goals, steps, tools, allies you are going to need accomplish that goal. Remember your adult goals:

A.D.U.L.T. Goals
A: stands for applicable (does it apply to your life)
D: stands for definable (specific and measureable)
U: stands for useful (beneficial)
L: stands for likely to happen (is this attainable)
T: stands for timetable (deadlines)

_____
_____
_____
_____
_____
_____
_____
_____
_____
_____
_____
_____
_____
_____
_____

Preparedness

Imagine, you're a super-secret spy and you were going after the CIA director. You followed him into a dry cleaner. However, you didn't have anything to protect your cover and your cover was blown. So, what does that mean for you my lovies? It means that if you aren't fully prepared for whatever situation you are about to enter, you will be screwed. Screwed in the sense that you will be exposed with no way to move forward.

Did you get everything you need for this course? You remember that Adulting Basics memo? Did you get everything? I hope you did (or at least begin the process of acquiring the items). There is nothing worse than being unprepared. There are many life circumstances in which those times will be needed. You want to hear a hilarious story of how I had my "cover blown" by not being prepared?!?

Of course you do:

I had just graduated from college and was looking for a job/career to start paying off my student loans. One of my best friends (hey bes fren!!!) had his mom hook me up with a job interview for a graphic designer position at the company where she worked. So, I'm going through the interview and when the interviewer asked the most important question: Can I see your portfolio? Guess who forgot her portfolio? Yeah, this girl right here!!! Like seriously...WHO DOES THAT?!?! Needless to say, I didn't get the job. Epic FAIL!!! But, a lesson learned!!! Since then, I have created both a physical and a digital online portfolio. Never again will I be caught without my "cover".

Please understand, preparedness is not only being materialistically prepared (having all the items you need) but also about being physically, mentally, spiritually, and emotionally prepared. Life, especially adult life, will throw you all types of curveballs and roundhouse kicks (at the same damn time even). You have to make sure you are geared up for the battles ahead...this is a war! You think I am joking ask any adult...we are constantly fighting to maintain our peace of mind, sanity, our aging bodies (you aren't gonna be young forever!), ourselves, and others.

Being prepared doesn't mean having all of the answers...it means having the peace of mind, the stillness in your heart, and the ability to walk with confidence in your truth through any situation. That takes time and practice. Practicing is a form of preparation. You have an interview, practice what you want to convey in the mirror. Study your mannerisms, tone, intonation, and verbiage.

Back in the day I used to be a girl scout. Girl Scouts organizations ALWAYS emphasized preparedness. So I am emphasizing that to you today. BE PREPARED... but what does that even mean?

Preparedness looks differently for each situation, however, the steps to preparedness are always the same: Know your situation, anticipate expectations, and act accordingly.

One must be prepared for the journey ahead...and for the randomness of life that one can't be prepared for, one must be grounded in GOD to pull strength from within to persevere!!!

Simple enough right?! Here are some examples:

A precursor for all of these scenarios: OWN YOUR SHIT!!! Be confident in who you are and what you know. This will help you get through the times in life where things don't go as planned.

Preparing for School

As a basic, make sure you have a pen or pencil and paper. Like seriously, DO NOT...I REPEAT DO NOT come to class without a way to write things down.

If you are in college, read the bloody syllabus!!! Like seriously, it is the roadmap to specific grades. You want to get an A, you know how much work and to what quality you need to do it in in order to get it.

If you are in middle/high school, come prepared for class like the teacher asks you to be. If you need a binder, get the binder...if you need a 3-subject notebook get the notebook.

If there are financial obstacles that are preventing you from acquiring the materials you need (this goes for all levels of education) talk to your teachers. I remember one semester in undergrad I couldn't afford the books I needed, I talked to all my professors and was able to borrow a copy of the books from them. It is better to have an older edition of the book than no book at all!!!

Preparing for Work

Preparing for work is similar to preparing for school. Have the supplies that you need, know the expectations of you, ask questions, and have the confidence that you belong there!

Most importantly, know the culture of your place of employment and dress accordingly. However, don't neglect who you are and your style. Work within the confines of that culture without forgetting your own. If your setting is extra professional but you are like me (jeans, sneakers, and a hoodie) then learn how to finesse that suit and tie to fit your relaxed style.

Preparing for Citizenry

So this is basically the how to be prepared for being an ACTIVE citizen. Not one of those I'm gonna talk shit about what is going on in society but do absolutely nothing about it except share my "rage" and "disgust" about it on the Twitters, Instagram, and Facebook. Yup, I'm probably talking about you and I don't care!!! So get up off your phone, tablet...put down this book (AFTER YOU FINISH READING IT) and be ACTIVE!!!

So first things first, REGISTER TO VOTE!!! Don't speak about it be about it. Next, read up on your local and state politicians. Make sure the people in office have YOUR best interest at heart. If it is an election year and a person is running who is in alignment with your principles, make sure you are assisting them to get elected. Put your money where ya mouth is!!!

This is 'Mur'kkka, money is the only motivator. Got any questions?!?! Follow me on twitter @begonia_says (hurry up, I need some followers...LOL) and we can tweet this out (I mean work this out) so you can be productive citizens of this here U S of A!!!

Preparing for Failure

Oddly enough, preparing for failure isn't that hard. We are innately geared to dealing with defeat and failure. But one thing to remember is to know that failure is a lesson and a blessing. Failure signifies that you actually did something. You applied yourself and tried something. Failure is part of the trial & error process. Now you know that that particular avenue, that particular methodology, that particular path does not work for you. That means that you need to figure out another method and/or another route to take you to success.

This thing called failure is just your next step towards success. So make sure you have your pen and pad so that you can write down and cross off those things, methods, steps, and paths that do not get you to where you want to be.

Preparing for Success

One of the hardest things you can do is prepare for success (as well as the perceived notions of success). Once you "Make It" there are a lot of expectations coming at you. Whether they are from family, friends, framily, frienemies, haters, and even self-imposed expectations. On the flip side, your success comes with expectations from yourself.

These expectations begin to form notions of perfectionism, expectations of failure, and even worse, the feeling of not deserving of the success you worked so hard to get...which all will drive you crazy and do nothing for your continued growth and success. So, what do you do to combat these thoughts and feelings.

Simple, create a mantra and every morning you look yourself in the mirror and say it or, if you're like me and have a soundtrack for feeling like a Badass. You play it and dance around your house until you are confident and you get your swagger back - do people say swagger anymore?

Another thing, with success comes exposure. You have to begin to mentally prepare yourself to have all eyes on you and what that means for you and your future. Are you going to be ready for the next steps? Do you have measures put into place to level up? Know that success will come and you will need to make sure you are prepared for it. This is where having your moral compass comes in handy. You will have the mental fortitude to deal with the pressures that come from having success.

And don't forget your morning motivational mantra.

Now this isn't meant to be an all-inclusive list of what to do to be prepared but it is meant to get you to think about your settings and what you might need to do to be successful in those settings!!!

Some quick notes:
Mentally prepare yourself for the following -
The immature, reckless, annoying, shiftless people you know in high school will be that way through college and adulthood. Some people never change.

Oh we aren't done yet -

NOTE TO (your)SELF:
<u>Always (and I do mean always) carry the following:</u>
- Pen
- Paper
- Facial tissue
- Hand sanitizer
- Umbrella
- $20 in cash (with at least $3 in change [the kind that makes noise])
- A way to contact someone (this also means memorizing some numbers)
- Lotion
- Lip moisturize
- Something to freshen your breath (Trust, you'll thank me later!!!)

Either way, preparation of the mind, body, spirit, and soul is the only thing that will get you through.

GET IT RIGHT, GET IT TIGHT:

Situation: You are going on a camping trip in (like inside, inside) the Grand Canyon (Arizona side). You will be there for a week (Wednesday to Wednesday). You invite your best friend. Your best friend has never been camping before, let alone in the Grand Canyon. Your best friend is asking you what to bring to be prepared.

Now it is preparation time. What are the suggestions that you will have for your best friend? What are some of the circumstances that can arise while being in the Grand Canyon? Don't be afraid of the Googles it can help you. You can also BING your way out of this one as well.

Your answer:

_____
_____
_____
_____
_____
_____
_____
_____
_____
_____
_____
_____
_____
_____
_____

#SquadGoals

Friends matter. Relationships matter.
Your inner circle matters.

I have always been very protective of my space. I don't care what title and/or relationship (friend, family, framily, foe, frenemy, etc.) you have with me, if you enter into my space with shenanigans you will find yourself exited out of my life quick, fast and in a hurry. You will find yourself bounced out, no questions asked...no explanations given!

There is a good and a bad side to this. The good side is that you only have positive vibes in your camp. The bad side is you might be the only person in your camp. You become so skeptical and jaded by the actions of others that you don't allow others into your camp.

I personally have always kept an extremely small circle. It was lonely at times, but thankfully I am ok with being with myself so I wasn't bored. But I knew I had goals I wanted to achieve and couldn't do that alone (no one is an island, success does not happen in a vacuum). So I decided to create my tribe. I took the qualities that I knew I needed help with and found them in others. And some found me.

I'm sure you are wondering: what do I even mean by that. Let me tell you about Reggie. So, I am chilling at the end of the bar by my lonesome (minding all of my own business). She is at the other end of the bar speaking with her friends. Why, I have no clue, she decides to include me in the conversation. And truthfully, we've been friends ever since. She has been a HUGE asset to my personal and professional growth and I am thankful for the happenstance.

Then there is Amber. Amber and I met through a mutual friend working on an amazing project. I gravitated towards her energy and we instantly became friends. Her friendship has allowed for this book to be written. She pushes me beyond the boundaries of my comfort zone.

There is the A-1, Day 1 - Alli. We go back since to the early 1980s. Our friendship was more like a familial relationship. We didn't always like each other but we ALWAYS had each other's back. We pushed each other to grow and even now we are pushing each other daily to move beyond our comfort zones so we are our best selves and living our best life. We not gonna talk about how I made her quit her job and it was the best decision of her life.

Then there is Ginger. Ginger is the even tempered, mild mannered person that makes me remember to always stay calm. Never lose your cool, never let them see you sweat. Although she has never said that, she lives that. She is also the person (along with Alli) who will let you know your decision was stupid but will still have your back while you realize how stupid your idea is. Contrary to what people say, you don't need YES'SIR friends. You need people who know and believe in your journey and who believe that you are greater than what you are showing yourself to be.

There are other people who I have had the pleasure of knowing across different times in my life. And who have been a part of my tribe. Your tribe does change as your life circumstances change and as you change locations. When I was in undergrad I had an amazing tribe! Although we are not as close as we used to, I will always hold a special place in my heart for them.

Ok, enough of all of that mushy stuff. You need people who not only will challenge you but sharpen the skills you already have. So get you a tribe, get you a squad. Remember these people can make or break you, so choose wisely.

> Proverbs 27:17 - "Just as iron sharpens iron, a person sharpens the character of his friend" (Complete Jewish Bible).

If you need assistance figuring out how to pick your tribe, let's work this out! Let's go back to Day 2 when we talked about the person you are and/or the person you want to be. When you are trying to BECOME, you have to have a tribe. People who will hold you accountable to the goals that you have set as well as the limitations that you have put on yourself.

A prime example of this is a conversation I witnessed between two gentlemen. Jon is building an empire through social entrepreneurship. One of Jon's biggest vices is alcohol. Carl was addressing Jon about that. Carl told Jon that because of the empire he is building and the way he is building it (though social entrepreneurship) he can't afford to drink. Carl further elaborated about accountability and how Jon isn't holding himself accountable for his own limitations (not drinking) and that he isn't surrounding himself with people who will hold him accountable. In addition to that, Carl asked Jon: what will he do if he isn't holding himself accountable, but he refuses to listen to people who are actually holding him accountable to his goals and his limitations.

Through this conversation, Carl was holding Jon responsible and accountable for his actions. One of those teachable moments in the moment.

In that same fashion, we must also reflect on what will our actions be when we are confronted with our own accountability partners. How will we respond when people hold us accountable but refuse to address and change our behaviors that are not conducive to our goals and limitations.

There is nothing worse than having a dope ass tribe and being the suckiest member in the tribe. The purpose of a tribe is for all of you to be able to strengthen and sharpen each other. My tribe, we rise together...POINT BLANK PERIOD!

The truth hurts but it will set you free. It will give you the freedom to know and grow. Make sure your tribe is doing that for you. But most importantly, make sure you are doing that for your tribe. Don't be the weakest link and don't be the reason your tribe leaves you in the past.

GET IT RIGHT, GET IT TIGHT:

I wish there was a **GET IT RIGHT, GET IT TIGHT** that I could give you to help you form your tribe, but there isn't. This is a trial and error process and it only comes with experience. Discernment is a huge part in moving towards having a solid tribe. Your tribe won't look like my tribe or move like Rihanna's tribe. You have to find what you need and what in you can add value to the lives of those in your tribe.

Instead this **GET IT RIGHT, GET IT TIGHT** is here to help you evaluate those that are around you and the benefits that they bring to you and what you bring to them.

Name: _____

I want to be:

_____
_____
_____
_____

They can help me with (by):

_____
_____
_____
_____
_____
_____
_____
_____

I can help them with (by):

_____
_____
_____
_____
_____
_____
_____
_____

Name: _____

I want to be:

_____
_____
_____
_____

They can help me with (by):

_____
_____
_____
_____
_____
_____
_____
_____

I can help them with (by):

_____
_____
_____
_____
_____
_____
_____
_____

Name: _____

I want to be:

_____
_____
_____
_____

They can help me with (by):

_____
_____
_____
_____
_____
_____
_____
_____

I can help them with (by):

_____
_____
_____
_____
_____
_____
_____
_____

Name: _____

I want to be:

_____
_____
_____
_____

They can help me with (by):

_____
_____
_____
_____
_____
_____
_____
_____

I can help them with (by):

_____
_____
_____
_____
_____
_____
_____
_____

Name: _____

I want to be:

_____
_____
_____
_____

They can help me with (by):

_____
_____
_____
_____
_____
_____
_____
_____

I can help them with (by):

_____
_____
_____
_____
_____
_____
_____

Advocacy

This chapter is going to seem harsh but it is necessary. There is no nice way to put this so it is going to be straight, no chasers. Understanding advocacy is a matter of life or death. This isn't that fake "life or death" this is true life or death. Not advocating for yourself with your doctor can lead to your death. Not advocating for yourself at a job can lead to financial death. Not advocating for yourself in relationships can lead to emotional and mental death. This is not a fucking drill...this is it, this is life! Shit is about to get REAL!!!!

Understand, advocacy is all about protecting yourself, your life, your character, your family, your everything (remember, LIFE OR DEATH)!!! Your advocacy plan is a weapon. Its effectiveness is dependent upon your ability to properly devise and execute a plan. Are you ready to use the greatest weapon you have at your disposal or are you gonna punk out, sit there and do nothing?

You are going to have to get up off your ass and gladiate for yourself. That is what advocacy is all about. Not feeling bad about yourself or your circumstances and making calculated moves to change your circumstances. This is not the time to cower like some scared puppy in the corner. It's time to put your big girl/boy pants on and put some bite to your bark. It's time for you and everyone to learn to put some RESPEKT on ya name!!!

Now is the time when you will have to stand on your own two feet. There won't be others there to make those important decisions/calls for you anymore. This my friend is not the time that you clam up and bitch up...this is the time you stand firm and press forward. You dig your heels in deep and you become unmovable and unstoppable and go for yours!!!

I know that these words seem harsh, it be that way sometimes. It is imperative that you understand the gravity of the situation. Advocacy is a key skill to have as an adult. You cannot and will not be successful unless you have begun to master this skill. Advocacy takes a lot of courage. It's more than just puffing up your chest and making demands. Advocacy looks different in different situations, but the results are the same, getting what you need and sometimes what you want.

What does all of this even look like? Why is it even necessary? It is necessary because no one will care about you like you do. No one will do for you like you. No one knows you like you do. SO YOU GOTTA LEARN TO DO FOR YOU!!!

Next are two different scenarios of advocacy, or at least having a seat at the table. Each situation was handled differently and you can see what it looks like when you properly advocate for yourself and when... you just became a punk!

Scenario 1:
There is a video of a little girl that always makes me chuckle (if you get a chance to watch it you should). The little girl is explaining to her mother why she doesn't like the particular hairstyle that her mother gave her. Her mom asks her, "You're making a choice for yourself?" and she responds, "Yes I am making a choice by myself...so I can have a better hairdo." Then her mom asks what she wants, the little girls response: TWIST IT! Even at that age, the little girl was advocating for herself. And not only did she express her dissatisfaction with her hairdo, she had a solution for it.

Scenario 2:
During a protest against police brutality a young man was arrested. After the arrest, the young man was given the opportunity to sit down with the mayor of his city, the police chief, and the president of city council - talk about having a seat at the grownup table. While at this meeting the young man continued to "protest" the unfair treatment and reiterated his disdain for police brutality. In the end, all he did was complain. There were no solutions that he brought to the table, thus no resolution to his issue.

These two scenarios let you see how advocacy can work for you or not advocating for yourself - or even others - can lead to a huge waste of time. As you can tell, scenario 1, although cute and funny, is exactly what you need to do. Even at that young age she was able to articulate in clear terms her problem and her solution to said problem. Being able to fend for yourself and having a solution to your issues is where you will need to get to. You can't just say I don't like this. You have to be able to say what you want in terms that seems like a win-win for the other party. Because let's be honest...no one wants to lose!

In the second scenario you see the greatest travesty of all time. There's nothing worse than having a seat at the table and squandering the opportunity through restating the problem and not coming up with a solution. What makes this situation worse is that in the future, he may never be given an opportunity to have a seat at the table (even if he is prepared to advocate) because that bad taste of ineffective communication that he brought to the table.

There is a preparation process that one must have in place in order to effectively and efficiently advocate for oneself. But know, this book has prepared you for this moment. Your ability to advocate for yourself is the culmination of all the skills you learned in this book. No matter the situation there will come a time where you will need to use your moral compass, your end-game strategy, and preparedness skills. You can't properly advocate for yourself without these skills.

You know how to figure out your end-game, prepare for all situations, even unexpected situations and most importantly, you have learned your moral compass and how to stand in your own truth. Any good training takes all previous skills and combines to make the most powerful weapon imaginable.

Your moral compass is going to be the guiding force to determine what is important and what is not. It will help you to decide when to go and when to stop. It will also help you decide which is the best tactic to use. Your moral compass will guide you to figuring out what you want the resolution to be. Although this is supposed to be a win-win for all involved, never forget that most importantly, YOU GOTTA WIN!!! But you can't win if you are not using your moral compass to guide you. So take that step back, take that breather and think. YES, THINK!!! Giving yourself a pause (or a break) allows you to purposefully look at the situation and make sure that the next steps you take are aligned with your moral compass. We are working on purposeful reactions and not off the cuff reactions that can ruin our character and our present and future successes.

After you have figured out what direction is best for you based on your moral compass, you must figure out your end game in order to come up with the best plan of action to achieve your solution. Figuring out your end game you can determine what you want and how you can go about getting it. In this process you will go backwards and forwards trying to figure out the best resolution/solution. Look at your paths from different angles to see how all the other parties involved will look at and receive your solution.

Now before you begin to prepare for your moment of advocation please, I beg of you PUH-LEASE!!! holla atcha tribe. Let your tribe be your sounding board. Let them, let you see the other viewpoints that you might have missed. Your tribe can help you come up with a better solution and/or help you with the preparation and execution of your plan. Moments like this are what you created your tribe for, so use them to help make you great!

Once you have consulted with your tribe and figured out what your game plan will be in order to advocate for yourself (and/or others) you will need to prepare yourself. Whether it is mentally, spiritually, physically, emotionally, financially (or whatever other 'ally' you need); it's game time and you need to get yourself together so when you step in or get your seat at the table you are ready to advocate.

When you are ready to advocate, walk into the situation with your head high and like you've already won. It's time to gladiate and know...no matter how the situation goes down, you've already won. Never forget your principles. During the advocation process tempers will flare, emotions can get high, remember... take a step back and keep your cool. You have a goal/objective...keep it at the forefront of your mind and your conversation. Most importantly, you also have a moral compass. Never let someone else's words or actions make you forget to check to make sure your moral compass is ALWAYS pointing to your principles.

So you think you got the juice you need to advocate for yourself? I know you do!!! It will take some time to get the audacity to cross lines, sit at tables you weren't invited to, and other forms of advocacy. As time progresses, you will get the faith, strength, courage, and wisdom to begin advocating throughout your life without breaking a sweat. It's okay to be nervous, that's only normal. Many people have anxieties about stepping out (myself included) but you, just like myself, will be A-OK. You got the stuff, just show em what ya working with and ya can't lose. You might have setbacks but you will not lose. Plug NAS's Ether in and repeat after me: I...WILL...NOT...LOSE!!!

Originally I was going to have you go back and help me redo my messy situation with my professor but that situation is so far in the past it doesn't even matter. Although, had I known then what I know now (hindsight is always 20/20), I would have done things much, much differently. Hell, had I had this book I could have done life differently. But you live and you learn, and you are lucky because you can live through my experiences and learn from them without screwing up your life. However, I want you to be great in these streets so I want you to practice on something that will get you some immediate rewards. At some point you will have to go into an interview. Your job in that interview is to not just get the job, but to get paid what you are worth (or a little more than what you are worth- but NEVER less).

So for this **GET IT RIGHT, GET IT TIGHT** we are going to work on getting paid. You like the sound of that?!? But wait...there's more. You remember how I said I was going to show you how to own your doctor visits?

Well this **GET IT RIGHT, GET IT TIGHT** has two situations to help you advocate for your financial and physical success.

Below is the quick steps to proper advocation. Use them to help you go through what you need to do to for each of the situations presented

    Figure out if this is a fight worth fighting

    End-Game Mentality: what do you want out of this situation

    Prepare: Who are your allies? What do you need to prove your point?

    Keep a level head, articulate your wants/needs/desires and suggested outcome/solution

    Stand in your truth

GET IT RIGHT, GET IT TIGHT:

Situation #1:

You see the position of a lifetime. You read over the job description and know you are the person for the job. Like you look at your past work experiences and you know these people would be foolish not to hire you. But then you look at the salary and your heart drops. You know for what they are asking you to accomplish in your role and what they want to compensate you for doing that role does NOT equate. Your job is to land an interview, convince them you are the candidate for the job, AND you need to be compensated more than what they are willing to give you.

Your answer:
Is this battle worth fighting: ___Yes ___No

What do I want out of the situation?

_____
_____
_____
_____
_____
_____
_____

Who are my allies?

_____
_____
_____
_____
_____
_____
_____

What is my course of action?

GET IT RIGHT, GET IT TIGHT:

Situation #2:
You haven't been feeling well lately. You have been very tired, your legs hurt and thanks to WebMD you suspect that you have a blood clot. You go to your doctor and your doctor is ignoring your suggestions that you might have a blood clot. You know you aren't crazy and you really wish that the doctor would take you seriously. What are you going to do to advocate for yourself to make sure the proper tests are done so you can be certain whether or not you have a blood clot and what can be done about it.

Your answer:
Is this battle worth fighting: ___Yes ___No

What do I want out of the situation?

_____
_____
_____
_____
_____
_____
_____

Who are my allies?

_____
_____
_____
_____
_____
_____
_____

What is my course of action?

Be You, ALWAYS

Hey Sweetie,

I know I don't know you personally...but I write this to you because I love you and I want nothing but the best for you. We have spent this time together and I have given you all the advice I can think of (for now). This wasn't meant to be an all-inclusive how-to book but a guide to get you started on this journey called YOUR LIFE. I know we shall meet again, another time, another book...but before we depart, I want to leave you with this one last piece of advice.

No matter what life throws at you...Be You, ALWAYS! Never forget who you are and/or who you want to be. That person must show up every day, that person can never take a day off. And when I mean never, I do mean NEVER. You can't let people catch you slippin'. Don't let people get you out of character. It takes a lifetime to build up your character and the blink of an eye to destroy it.

You have to show up every day and in every way. There is no point of being you if you are always going to mold yourself based on your surroundings. We aren't in the business of being chameleons. You aren't trying to turn colors to fade into the background. You are here to be you: if you are a tiger why change your stripes for someone else...if you are a wolf why rock the sheep's clothing? There is one thing to adapt you to your surroundings and it's quite another to change you for your surroundings.

It will take some time getting the wisdom to know when to turn you down and when to turn you up... but never, and I do mean NEVER, by any means turn you OFF! You gotta be on, you gotta be you, you just gotta...no IFs, ANDs, or BUTs about it!!! So...Be You, ALWAYS! and you can never go wrong!!!

Now let's not get all fairytale-ish. There will be times where you will have to decide to go with your core principles or follow the crowd. There will be times when your core principles are put to the test and you are challenged to the point you want to abandon them. Life is crazy like that. But don't give up on who you are and who you want to become. Stay true to you...Be You, ALWAYS!

When you are doing what you need to progress towards a better you, there will be times where you aren't able to do like others do or do what others do. You are now in a league all of your own. You are on a road to be the greatest you ever, and one major misstep can change your trajectory forever. I am not suggesting that you try to live a perfect life because that is impossible and unreasonable. However, I am suggesting that you make your choices based on your moral compass and not on whims and desires. You don't want to be in a position where people are quoting Jay-Z: WE DON'T BELIEVE YOU, YOU NEED MORE PEOPLE! You are your first source for advertisement of who you are (or who you are becoming). People need to believe you before they can believe others about you.

Trust and believe people will try to test you and your character. They will try to see if what you say matches what you do. I remember a while back, I decided to do a year of sobriety. People thought it was a joke. At that point in my life I was knocking em back like shots of water. So to hear that the turn up queen was stepping down was just crazy to people. One time I had a person try to pour liquor down my throat because they thought it was all a joke. I stepped back and said you gonna break the rules of drinking and waste this alcohol. After that day, no one tested me nor did they question me. People will begin to believe the changes you are making as long as you are consistent. Consistency is the key to change.

But not being willing to maintain consistency, not wanting to control yourself...not being you, ALWAYS leads to some very devastating consequences. I've seen way too many times where people get reckless because of lack of self-control and wind up hurting themselves and the empires they wish to build. Don't be that person, don't miss your blessings because of your vices and recklessness. Don't ruin what you have worked so hard to change. Don't worry about what other people are doing or how they are feeling while you are on the road to being the best you!!!

Remember...this is your life. Do it your way!!!

Never forget, walk with purpose. Enter every space you go into like GOD rolled out the red carpet for you and the angels have introduced you to the world. Hold your head up high. Never be ashamed of your mistakes or missteps...they created the path for you to be right where you are. Because what would your life be like without them? I know my life would be totally different without mine, and I wouldn't have been able to give you all this great advice - and what would your life be like without knowing all this great advice?!?!

Know that this path is yours and yours alone. Many times people will try to have you walk the path that they want for you. Or even worse, the path that they wish they had gone down. But let me tell you, stand strong in your resolve to live your life on your terms. Be you, ALWAYS!!!! This is your life to live your way and no one, and I do mean NO ONE should take that away from you. Do NOT let them, don't give someone that power to lead you down the path that is not yours.

This is your life, live it on your terms...POINT, BLANK, PERIOD!!!! No questions!!!

Thank you for taking the time to read this book. I truly hope that not only did you learn some great information but, that you also had fun along the way. Get a head start on this adulting thing and rock out.

Love Always,

Sonia B.

Sonia Begonia

PS: We shall talk soon! But I am so glad you got **THE MEMO!!!**

|